*Black's Picture Sports*
# RIDING

*Black's Picture Sports*
# RIDING
*Sports Illustrated · Revised by*
Patsy Arnold

Adam and Charles Black · London

This edition first published 1976 by A & C Black Ltd
35 Bedford Row, London WC1R 4JH

ISBN 0 7136 1613 X

Cover and photos on pages 8–9, 14, 24, 30, 31, 60, 61, 77,
78, 94 Leslie Lane; 12 Jerry Cooke; 92 Richard Lerner

Authorised British edition
© 1976 A & C Black Ltd
Originally published by J B Lippincott Company in the
United States of America as *Sports Illustrated Horseback
Riding* by the Editors of Sports Illustrated © 1971
Time Inc (revised)

Set and printed in Great Britain by
Page Bros (Norwich) Ltd, Norwich

# Contents

5

# 1 Introduction

## RIDING MUST BE FUN

More people of all ages are riding for pleasure today than at any time since the car replaced the horse. You can learn to ride whether you are six or sixty. The age at which you begin is not important, and the common belief that you will never be a good rider unless you start as a child is erroneous. But what is important is the manner in which you set about learning. If you proceed slowly and correctly you will learn to ride well and your pleasure wiil be greatly enhanced. To learn properly you should have a well-behaved horse and supervision. Both are normally obtainable at riding stables. You will find also that an advance understanding of what you and the horse do, separately and together, will make learning much easier. That is the purpose of this book.

Riding is an all the year round sport that offers endless variety. You do not need a partner or a group to enjoy it. A solitary ramble can be as pleasant as a jaunt with friends.

You *do* need to be able to manage your horse. Do not be misled by well-intentioned friends who tell you that there is nothing at all to riding and that you can teach yourself without any trouble. You are likely to spend several unhappy hours and form a number of bad habits before you are convinced to the contrary. For example, you may find yourself invited to join a group of experienced riders who tell you that your horse will follow quietly. Perhaps he will—but at a variety of speeds that

7

could make the trip pretty horrifying – and perhaps dangerous.

## LEARNING THE RIGHT WAY

If you go off alone and hire a horse without previous instruction, the stable may give you an animal which is familiar with the ways of inexperienced riders. In the ring old Nellie may simply march to the centre and stand quietly dozing for an hour. Out of doors she may head off amiably for the park only to stop and eat grass at the first likely-looking spot, returning you safely when your money's worth of time is used up. Save your money and your temper, swallow your pride and learn correctly. Nellie will give you a great ride when you know how to ask her.

Most areas have riding schools; consult your friends or your classified directory. Most will offer either private or group lessons; but not all of them, either in the city or the country, will offer both. The quality of instruction will, of course, vary. If you have a choice, spend a day or so just watching at the school you like best. You can observe just how much attention the instructor gives the student, and in which manner it is given. Consider too the physical aspects of the establishment. An indoor ring means you can ride in all kinds of weather and at night. These advantages will not outweigh learning to ride outside, which is ultimately essential both for your confidence and ability to control your mount.

These days you must only go to an establishment licenced by the local council and then preferably to one which has been approved of by the British Horse Society. The BHS ensures that the standard of care of the horses and ponies is satisfactory, and keeps a check also on the suitability of the instruction at various levels. It is not necessary to go to the best instructor when you start learning so long as you make certain that the basics are really well taught. There are unfortunately some estab- lishments still in existence which do not have proper qualifications, and these are to be avoided. All those which are licenced and approved will display the relevant sign.

## PRIVATE LESSONS

It is preferable to start with private lessons. These may seem expensive but they represent money well spent in terms of pleasure, safety and achievement of competence. Private instruction is essential for small children and timid adults. It is best to begin by taking several half-hour lessons a week. Then, as your muscles become attuned, you can increase the length of the lessons. After about ten hours of private instruction, the average person is usually able to start, stop and turn a horse, rise to the trot and have some idea about sitting the canter. The degree of skill acquired will, of course, depend on the individual, but *no one* is an expert rider at this stage. To become one will take considerable time and a good deal of work.

## UNDERSTANDING HORSES

There is no need to be afraid of horses, but you should be careful when with them. If you have never known a horse 'personally' before, approach him with an open mind. Do not be influenced by the behaviour of humanised television horses and do not think horses are like dogs — a horse is not an overgrown, loyal Rover. He is a horse and as such has his own unique character and individual personality. And despite romantic legends, it is reassuring to remember that horses are not as clever as people. Care and not fear is the sensible attitude: most accidents are due to ignorance on the part of the rider. To cite just one hazard: in getting acquainted with your horse it is quite correct to offer him a piece of apple or carrot – but put it on the palm of your hand and hold your hand out flat. He will take it very nicely. If you hold it in the tips of your fingers you may lose a few.

11

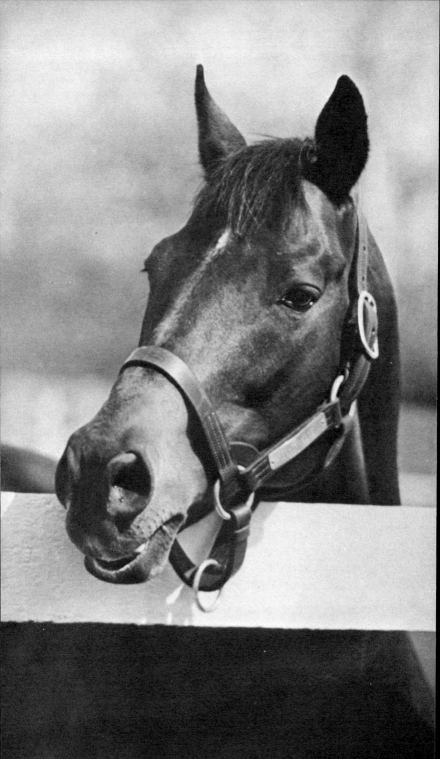

Don't expect your first horse to resemble the glamorous animals of films and television. Remember that handsome is as handsome does. Reliable stables usually supply beginners with horses which have been mellowed by age – there is a saying that a green horse and a green rider make a very bad combination.

How to lead your horse

14

# 2 Horse and Tack

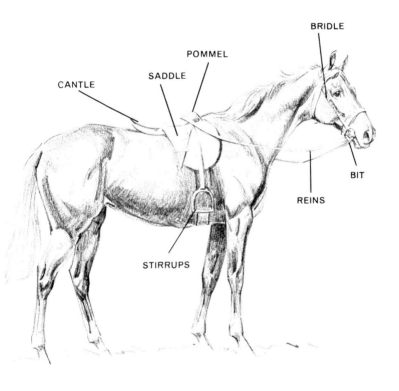

BRIDLE

POMMEL

SADDLE

CANTLE

BIT

REINS

STIRRUPS

Figure 1. The tack

# THE HORSE

It is not necessary to know the name of every part of a horse's anatomy and of all the equipment he wears before you start riding. However, a little advance familiarity with the language will make it easier for you to follow the text of this book. The drawings identify most of the terms you will hear while you are learning to ride.

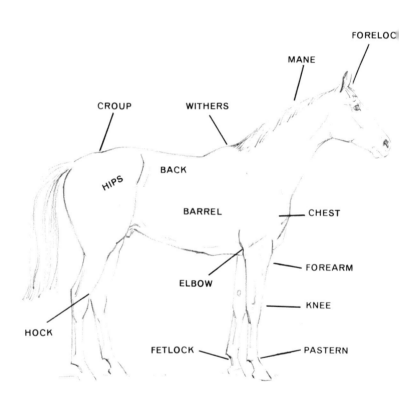

Figure 2. The horse's anatomy

16

# THE TACK

Let's start with the saddlery the horse wears—the 'tack', as horsemen call it. It will be helpful to know how and why it is constructed as it is and to see why it works the way it does. You will notice in the drawing that a standard

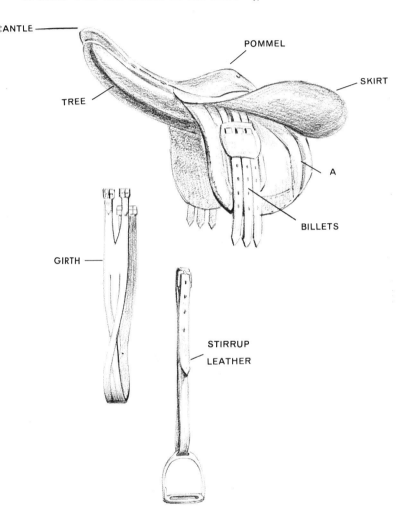

CANTLE

POMMEL

SKIRT

TREE

A

BILLETS

GIRTH

STIRRUP
LEATHER

Figure 3. The saddle, girth and stirrup

B

saddle is composed of several layers, each with a specific function. All saddles are made round a basic frame called the tree. This is made either of steel or more often in modern days, of fibre-glass, which as we know is very tough. The girth is the strap (leather, linen or cord) that is used to secure the saddle to the horse; it is buckled to straps on the saddle which are know as billets. Flap A protects the horse's side from being pinched by the buckles, and also from the horse's sweat. The stirrup is attached under the circular Flap C, and hangs down on the outside of the skirt. The stirrup leather has a buckle for lengthening or shortening. It should be slipped up under the flap after the length is adjusted. The leather is hung on a catch with either an open end or a hinged end (see Figure 4). This is called a safety catch, and if pressure is applied to the rear of the catch the stirrup leather will drop off. Thus, if a rider's foot is caught in the stirrup when he falls, he cannot be dragged; always check that this works.

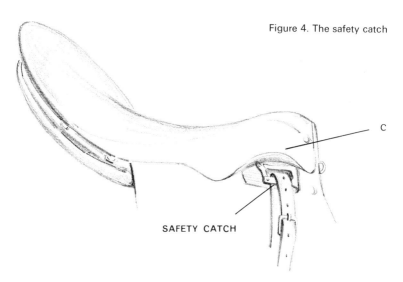

Figure 4. The safety catch

C

SAFETY CATCH

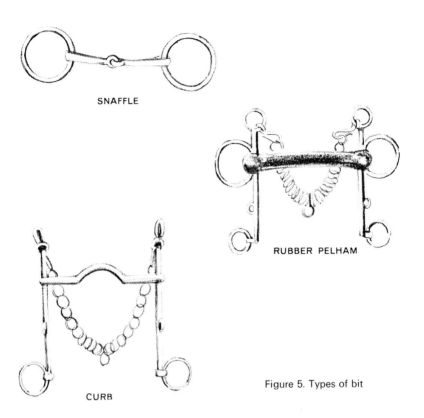

SNAFFLE

RUBBER PELHAM

CURB

Figure 5. Types of bit

The bridle is composed of a headpiece, a browband, a cavesson, cheekpieces, bits and reins. A horse's mouth has a gap between the front incisors and rear molars, and the bit (or bits) fits through the gap, resting across the tongue. There are many types of bit, but the basic ones are:

1 The snaffle, a straight bar hinged in the centre and requiring only one set of reins.

2 The pelham, which is a single — but one with a short shank and a slight port, and curb strap or chain. This requires two sets of reins.

19

3  The curb, a more severe bit, with a higher port, a longer shank and curb or chin, which is almost always used in conjunction with a snaffle. With this combination of two separate bits there are, of course, two sets of reins. Pulling on the reins applies pressure on the sides of the horse's lips and his tongue. With a properly fitted curb, the pressure extends to the roof of his mouth, and via the curb strap or chain, against the back of his chin.

## GENERAL TERMS

If you have studied all the drawings, you now should know the difference between a horse's withers and, say, his fetlock. Here are a few more general terms which will help you to feel knowledgeable when you arive for your first ride.

A filly is a female horse under the age of four – and, in registered breeds, all birthdays are counted as January 1, regardless of the actual date. After a filly's fourth birthday, she is called a mare. A male horse is a colt until he is four; then he becomes a horse unless he has been castrated, in which case he is a gelding. Most male riding horses are geldings.

(The age of an unregistered filly, mare, colt, horse or gelding can be determined by her or his teeth, which is why the mouth is not the place to look a gift horse in.)

Horses come in an assortment of colours, some with special names. A black or brown horse is called just that. However, a brown horse (ranging in colour from a light to a rich mahogany shade) with a black mane, tail and legs is called a bay. A horse of a brilliant  red-gold orange-copper or dark liver colour (or any reddish-brown colour) is called a chestnut – and occasionally a sorrel.

Most white horses are really faded greys. Grey horses are usually born black, with black skins; as they get older they get progressively whiter. A true white horse has a pink skin.

20

Then there are two-tone ones – roans, which are horses with a thick sprinkling of white hair through their coats – particularly bay, strawberry or chestnut. Spotted horses can be brown and white (skewbald), black and white) (piebald) or calico (bay and white – i.e. black, brown and white). The palomino – gold with a white mane and tail – is a breed as well as a colour, as is the Appaloosa (any colour, but with spots on his hindquarters). There are other variations of colour and on any of them may be white markings – stars, strips, blazes, and snips on the face, or stockings, socks, or coronets on the legs.

You will soon find that horses have as much individuality as people, in their colour, confirmation and personality, and before long you will smile condescendingly when some non-rider says: 'All horses look alike to me!'

Figure 6. Riding gear

# 3 Equipment and Seats

## WHAT YOU SHOULD WEAR

When you are learning to ride, dress simply and comfortably. It is essential to have a hard hat which may be covered in a variety of material, but which must fit exactly if it is to do the job for which it is designed. The next most important part of your clothing is a pair of jodphurs, stretch nylon is probably the most satisfactory material. These need not be expensive. A pair of boots will be required; whereas a few years ago these would normally have been short leather or jodphur boots, nowadays long ones made of rubber are popular, serviceable and moderately priced. It is sensible to wear a jacket over a jumper or shirt, and you can either purchase a proper tweed hacking jacket or continue with one you already have. Finally a pair of gloves will complete your outfit – these will prevent blisters if worn regularly.

## RIDING STYLES

There are several different styles of riding, some for highly specialised work and others which may be temporarily fashionable. Rising is largely a matter of balance and control, and if you have been properly taught the basics of handling yourself and the horse at a walk, trot and canter, you will find no difficulty in varying your style later should you want to.

The basic seat

Holding the reins – correct position

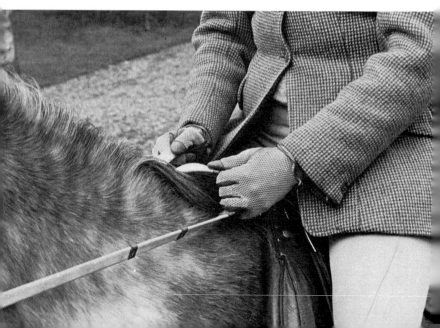

# POSITION IN THE SADDLE

*Position* is the foundation of proper horsemanship. Your correct position and posture in the saddle and on the horse can and should be learned at a standstill. Keep your head up and your eyes ahead; keep your back straight but not stiff, and your hands and arms flexible. Your seat and thighs are in close contact with the horse. The position of the foot in the stirrup and the length of the stirrup vary with the style of saddle and horse, but a study of the drawings of the main riding styles will show that these maxims are common to all of them. The main riding styles include:

1   The basic seat (Figure 7).
2   The Hunter seat—stirrups just a trifle shorter, body slightly more forward (Figure 8).
3   The dressage seat—stirrups longer (Figure 9).
4   The Western stock-horse seat – the reins held in one hand, the left, as horses are taught to turn by pressure on the neck (Figure 10).

Figure 7. The basic seat

Figure 8. The hunter seat

Figure 9. The dressage seat

Figure 10. The Western stock-horse seat

Mounting sequence. Note position of the crop in the rider's hand

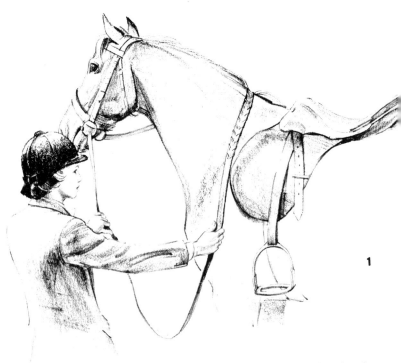

**1**

Figure 11. Arranging the reins

**2**

# 4 How to Ride

## ON THE GROUND

Attendants at livery stables and riding schools will often try to lead your horse up to a mounting block and summarily lift you on. Don't let them. There is more to horsemanship than riding, and correct ground procedure should be learned first. A horse is traditionally approached and led from his left side, which is also known as the near side. Get to know your horse by walking up beside his left shoulder and grasping the reins about 15 cm from the bit. Then, facing the same way as the horse, walk slowly forwards. Look straight ahead – not at the horse. He will walk beside you or behind you – not on you. In this position you are safe from kicks and bites and still have control of the animal. The closer you stand to the horse the safer you are – even the quietest will sometimes kick at a fly and hit you if you are in the way. There is no reason to be frightened of your horse, but that does not mean you should take him for granted. Any horse is capable of inflicting injury, but most accidents are the result of the rider's carelessness or ignorance.

It is most important to keep control of the horse at all times, and this is best done by keeping a firm hand on the reins. Now that you have walked your horse you are ready to mount. The first thing to do is get the reins in order. They are of equal length, and there is a seam or buckle which marks the centre spot. Find that seam and with the right hand pull the rein so that the slack is taken up on the off side. Then bring the left hand up

c

until it meets the right rein on the horses's neck just in front of the withers, and take both reins in the left hand. Be sure that the ends of the reins are neatly arranged alongside the shoulder of the horse so as not to get caught in the stirrup (see Figure 11).

# MOUNTING

In arranging the reins in your left hand, you have shifted the position of your body so that you are facing slightly to the rear. Your left hand (with the reins in it) should be resting easily on the horse's neck, about 10 cm ahead of the pommel (placing your hand too close to the pommel can result in pinched fingers). Now, without letting go of the reins, open the fingers of your left hand far enough to get a grip on the horse's mane. This will give you more stability and will stop you jerking the horse's mouth if at first you find yourself using the reins as a strap with which to pull yourself up. Take the top of the stirrup in your right hand and turn it towards you, then thrust your left foot all the way into it – 'home', as horsemen say – so that the metal is against the heel of your boot (1).

You are now ready for two forceful movements – a hop followed by a spring. The hop off your right foot will swing you round to face the horse and enable you to grasp the cantle of the saddle with your right hand. The spring, also off your right leg, follows immediately. With a good spring an adult can stand up straight in the left stirrup, but if you are shorter, like the girl illustrated here, you will have to pull with your arms as well. Your left hand drops a bit as you pull yourself up – but there is no change in the tension of the reins (2 and 3). While performing this manoeuvre keep the toe of your left foot – the one in the stirrup – pointed downwards and your leg close in to the horse. Otherwise you may nudge the horse in his side with the toe of your boot.

So now you are halfway there. Your weight is distributed between your arms and your left leg. Now lean on

Figure 12. Mounting—sequence

2

3

4

5

your left arm and move your right hand from the cantle
to the off, or right hand, side of the pommel (4). At the
same time swing your right leg over the horse's back
and let yourself down into the saddle. Hey presto! You're
up. Then place your right foot in the stirrup, take the
reins in both hands and you are ready to ride. The
process we have described here actually takes only about

37

Figure 13. Mounting—view from above

10 seconds, but you will need to practise it a good many times to make all the motions smooth. Don't be discouraged if it seems awkward at first. Even a small girl, as these illustrations show, can learn to mount an average-sized horse easily – and without any assistance.

Figure 13 illustrates mounting, as viewed from above, showing the position of your right hand after it has been moved from the cantle. The rider has not yet let herself down into the saddle. Note that her right ankle is cocked to help her leg clear the horse.

38

Figure 14. Up in the saddle

# GETTING A LEG UP

Once you have learned to mount a horse unassisted, it is permissible to allow an instructor or friend to 'give you a leg up'. For this procedure, you again take the reins in your left hand and grasp the mane just in front of the withers. Place your right hand on the cantle, and stand close to and facing the side of the horse. Bend your left leg at the knee so your helper can grip it, as shown in Figure 15. Then comes a combined and coinciding effort – you spring off your right foot and your helper pushes you upwards, keeping your left leg and knee pressed close to the saddle. The lift must be high enough to allow your right leg to swing clear of the croup. Your right hand moves on the saddle as when mounting unassisted. Always lower yourself into the saddle gently, not with a bump.

Figure 15. Getting a leg up

# DISMOUNTING

Now that you are in the saddle, your next move — before the horse ever takes a step — is to get out of it. Dismounting is very much like mounting, only in reverse. Gather the reins in your left hand and place them on the horse's neck.

Figure 16. Dismounting—sequence

Next, place your right hand below the pommel, remove your right foot from the stirrup and pass your right leg over the horse's back without touching it.

Shift your right hand to the cantle and keep the weight of your body on your hands. Remove your left foot from the stirrup and slide gently to the ground.

Even when descending, you should be in a position to maintain control of the horse. Don't push yourself away from the animal, but slide down his side. Note the position of the right hand and arm. If the horse moves, you can shift your weight to that arm and have your left hand free to prevent movement.

44

Figure 17. Preparing to ride

# PREPARING TO RIDE

Having learned to mount and dismount, you are ready to start riding. But first you need to understand the proper arrangement and balance of the various parts of your body – in a word, position. You can achieve the proper position to be used in motion while the horse is standing still – it is basically the same for the walk, the trot, the canter. As already stated, this is what you must do: keep your head up and eyes ahead; keep your back straight but not stiff and your hands and arms flexible; your elbows should be bent, with the reins held in front of the horse's withers, hands about 5 cm apart, and high enough to make a straight line from the horse's mouth to your elbows. Your seat and thighs should be in close contact with the horse, the ball of each foot in the stirrup, with the heel down.

# HOLDING THE REINS

Ordinarily you should keep both hands on the reins. However, occasions may arise when it is necessary to hold them in one hand—the left. Figure 18 shows how to hold the single rein, or snaffle, in both hands or in one. Figure 19 shows how to handle double reins. The top rein is still the snaffle, and the second is called the curb. Draw the snaffle through the palm of your hand. Hold it firmly between your thumb and the middle joint of your forefinger. To transfer the rein from your right hand to

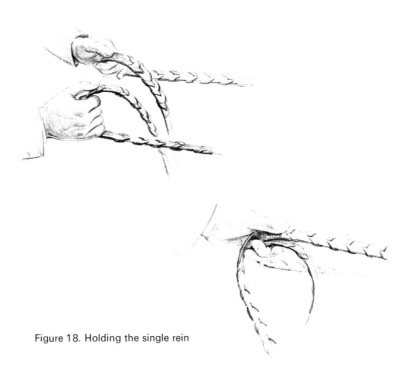

Figure 18. Holding the single rein

Figure 19. Holding double reins

your left, pass your right hand behind and under the left
and slip the rein into the palm of your hand.

To hold the double reins, loop the snaffle around your
little finger. Loop the curb rein around your second and
third fingers, holding both between the first and second.
To shift double reins, place your right hand behind the
left and slip your left forefinger between the snaffle and
the curb reins.

49

Figure 20. Using the crop

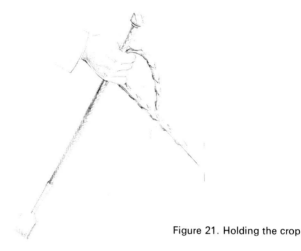

Figure 21. Holding the crop

## USING A CROP

You will not need to use a crop until you are ready to trot or canter, so for the sake of clarity we have not in general shown one in the rider's hand. The crop is an aid, as are your voice and legs, to urge the horse onwards. Not all horses need to feel a crop; for some, simply seeing one in the rider's hand is enough inspiration. You will note that the crop is carried in the right hand, as are the reins on occasion (Figure 20). If you need to use it, take the reins in your left hand (Figure 21), making sure that you have and can maintain control. Then use your crop briskly behind the girth.

51

Figure 22. Adjusting the saddle

## ADJUSTING YOUR EQUIPMENT

If you feel your saddle slipping, stop. Put your left leg in front of the saddle on the horse's shoulder, with your weight in the right stirrup and the reins in your right hand. Fold the skirt of the saddle forward under your calf, as shown below, or over your thigh. Take hold of a billet and pull upwards, past the hole you want, then let it slip back into position. Do the same thing with the other billet, making sure that both billets are flat when you have finished (Figure 22). To shorten or lengthen the stirrup

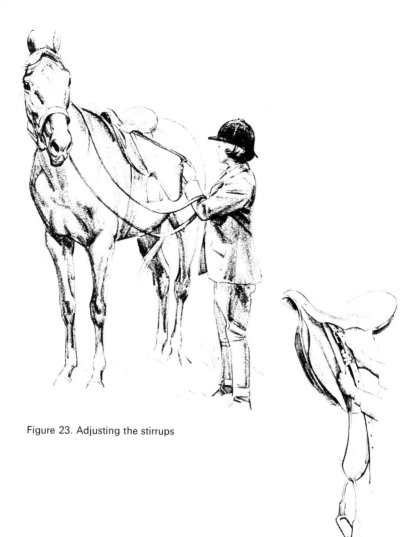

Figure 23. Adjusting the stirrups

before mounting, loop the reins around your left arm, then reach up under the flap and pull the buckle downwards. After adjusting to the proper length, check to see that the buckle is fastened; then pull downwards on the understrap and the buckle will slide into place.

Figure 24. Stopping and backing

# STOPPING AND BACKING

Stopping a walking horse is easy, once you know how to. (Actually, the type of horse you will be riding at this stage requires little encouragement to stop.) When you are ready, close your hands on the reins; the little fingers exert a squeezing action which increases the pressure on the reins and so on the horse's mouth. This alone may bring him to a halt, but if it does not you should increase the pressure. When your horse has stopped, try backing him. Use your hands in the same manner as you did when pulling to a halt from a walk. You will feel the horse's weight shift from the fore to the hindquarters before he starts moving into reverse. Give him time to make that shift. He will back a few steps. Ease off the pressure when he has stopped. That is his reward.

## AT THE WALK

Now you are ready to move, but before you do you must know several things about controlling your horse once he is in motion. You start and then maintain control by the proper use of the natural aids, which are your hands, your legs – and your seat. To start with, hold the reins

56

Figure 25. At the walk

lightly but firmly, so that you have a direct, 'feelable' contact with the horse's mouth. Nudge your horse gently with your legs – do not kick – and he will begin to walk. Use your legs to prevent the horse from stopping and your hands to restrain him from moving into a faster gait.

# GUIDING YOUR HORSE

The next thing to learn is how to steer your horse so that you can ride where you and not he, want to go. At first you will feel a terrible temptation to look down at yourself and the horse—just as a novice dancer wishes to watch his feet. Don't do it. Look ahead at where you are going; this not only helps to keep you in the correct position, but when you turn your head in the direction you wish the horse to go the subtle change in your weight helps direct him. By doing these things right you will set the scene for the use of your most important aid—the reins. By holding these evenly in both hands you have a light contact with the horse's mouth. Now to turn left pull your left hand slightly towards your body, thus putting more pressure on the left side of the horse's mouth. (To oversimplify slightly; if the horse's head is facing the way you want to go, the rest of the horse will follow. A well-schooled horse does not need to have his head pulled around, but occasionally the beginner will encounter one with an active interest in returning to his stable to munch hay. You can stop him. Keep aiming him where *you* want to go.) Try your turns first in the simplest manner, at a walk both to the right and to the left. Next, try circles to the right and left. Be sure you keep looking in the direction you want to go.

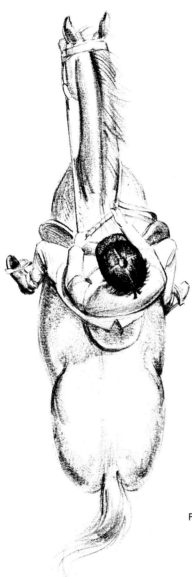

Figure 26. Guiding your horse

Rising to the trot

Sitting the canter

Figure 27. Rising to the trot

# RISING TO THE TROT

Once you have mastered yourself and your horse at the walk and are able to turn, stop and back, you are ready to progress to the next gait: the trot. The up-down movement which you must learn is often misunderstood. It is no affectation but an aid and confort to both horse and rider. When a horse trots, his legs move in diagonal pairs, making a two-beat rhythm as the hoofs hit the ground. The forward propulsion, or push — both for the horse and you — comes from *behind*, which is important to understand as it affects your movements and position in the saddle at all times. To start the gait use your legs or heels — your horse will go from a walk into a slow trot. For a few moments just sit there letting your knees and ankles act as shock absorbers. You will feel a bump, bump against your backside as the pairs of hoofs hit the ground, pushing or jolting you out of the saddle. Now using these same leg aids, urge your horse into a faster trot. The jolt is far more pronounced, and you will thump your saddle at a more rapid rate as those diagonal pairs of hoofs hit the ground faster and faster.

Time to start rising. This is what that means: when a pair of legs moves forward you are pushed forwards and upwards by the movement. You help by using your muscles, particularly your thigh muscles, to hold yourself in the air while the hoofs strike the ground, thus avoiding the jolt, then you let yourself down so you can be pushed forward and up again (see Figure 28). You will note from the drawings that you do not stand up in the stirrups or heave yourself out of the saddle. Actually, the horse does most of the work by providing the push while you practise to develop timing and coordination. Obviously, it is possible to rise with either pair of legs; you may be described as being on the right or left diagonal. To change diagonals simply sit through one bounce and catch the next push up. You're then on the opposite diagonal.

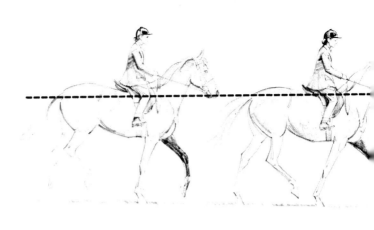

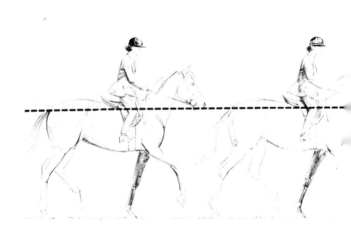

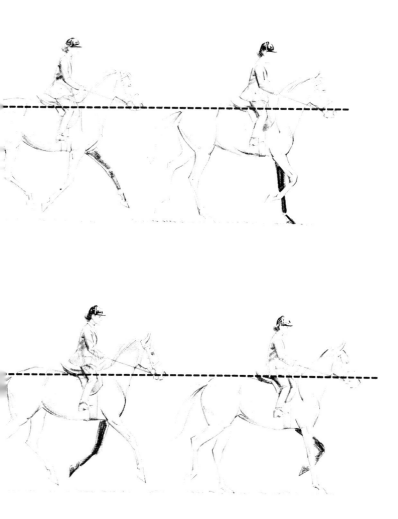

Figure 28. Rising to the trot—sequence

The blackened foreleg indicates how you can tell which diagonal you are rising with, by watching the horse's shoulder. If you are down when the right shoulder is back, then you are on the right diagonal. Note also the bounce of the horse, indicated by the broken line, as all four feet leave the ground at the trot's fullest extension. (Don't be confused: right or left does not mean right or wrong.)

65

E

Starting to rise you move forward and up from your original position (*dotted line*) as the horse goes into a trot. The forward motion of the horse's hind legs gives you the push that helps make rising less of an effort and more comfortable for the rider.

Figure 29. Starting to rise

At the peak of the rise, your seat is well off the saddle as the diagonal pairs of hoofs strike the ground, thus sparing you the jolt of the impact. Your knee is the hinge and, along with your ankle, provides you with a natural shock absorber.

Figure 30. At the peak of the rise

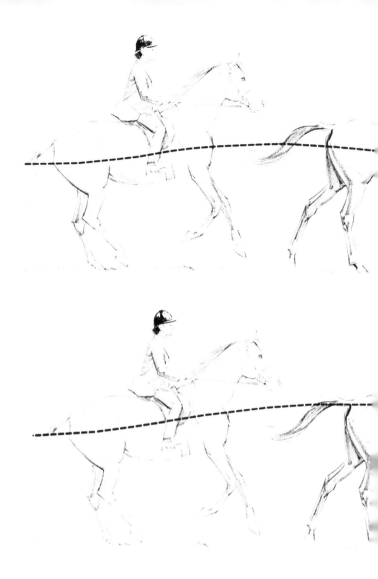

## SITTING THE CANTER

You have learned how to get yourself *out* of the saddle when rising to the trot; now it is time to learn how to stay *in* the saddle at the canter. The canter is the third of the natural

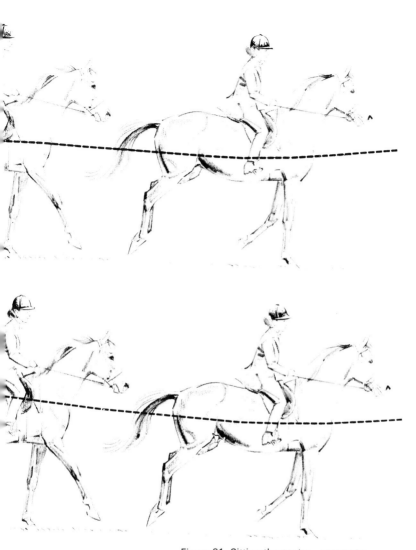

Figure 31. Sitting the canter—sequence

gaits of the average horse and is traditionally described as a three-beat gait. Figure 31 shows a simplified version of what happens when a horse is cantering. Notice that he starts out on the left hind foot, rolls onto his left front and right rear foot, then onto his right front foot. (Of

Figure 32. Sitting the canter

course, this pattern of footfalls can be executed in reverse, starting with the right hind foot etc. This is known as cantering on different leads, as one of the front legs seems to be leading the movement.)

You can make your horse canter either by urging him on from a slow trot or, with some horses which have

been trained to canter from a walk, by turning his head slightly and shifting your weight over the opposite shoulder. Once he is cantering, *relax*. Stiffening your backbone or pushing down into the stirrups will send you bouncing out of the saddle. You probably will pound the saddle for the first few strides while you adjust to the

Figure 33. Relaxed seat while cantering

new rhythm and the impression of speed. But once you are moving with the horse you will find this rolling movement of the canter the greatest pleasure to ride. If at this time (or any other time in riding) you should lose your stirrup *don't* look down to try to find it.

Keep your eyes looking ahead at where you are going, and doing this will in turn help you keep your balance. Keep your foot in position and you probably will catch your stirrup without difficulty. If you have mastered these two lessons, you should be capable of riding a well-trained horse safely and comfortably.

At the canter you will find that the upper part of your body is slightly more forward than at the walk. If you move from a trot to a canter remember to come down to a slow, sitting trot and also to use your legs to urge the horse to change gaits.

Remember, close contact with the saddle is necessary at the canter. Also notice that the turning principles at a faster gait are the same as at the walk. Using the reins, the rider should look in the direction of the turn, applying a light leg pressure to aid his horse.

Once you have mastered the skills outlined above, your thoughts will naturally turn to the thrills of galloping your horse over a long stretch of ground. It is not part of the scope of this book, however, to cover the techniques necessary for this advanced riding – or indeed of those for jumping your horse over hedges and ditches, either in the field or in the arena. This book is primarily concerned with helping you to acquire the basic riding skills – learn these well, then you will be ready to tackle more advanced riding.

Adjusting the saddle whilst still mounted

Cleaning the hoof

# 5 The Care and Feeding of Horses

## HOW TO BUY AND KEEP A HORSE

Now you have mastered the basic elements of riding and may be thinking of buying a horse of your own. Do seek the help and advice of someone who really knows horses, and also your own capabilities and temperament. If you are buying a horse for pleasure, it should be just that — a pleasure to ride and own. It can be of any breed – its ancestry does not matter. You could buy your horse at an auction. This can be exciting, but is often unsatisfactory, unless you are very knowledgeable and experienced in this form of buying. Be sure to examine any apparent bargain carefully; there is often as good a reason for a low price on a horse, as there is on a cheap second-hand car!

A riding horse reaches maturity by the time he is seven years old. However, do not be sceptical about buying a mount with 'a little age on him', as long as he is sound and is *well-mannered*. An experienced horse can teach an inexperienced rider a lot. A ten- or twelve-year-old horse, if he has been properly treated, should have a good deal of life left. Many horses have been hunted, a vigorous activity, until late in their teens or even early twenties. Care and condition, past, present and future, will determine the span of usefulness – barring drastic accidents, of course.

**Behaviour of the horse**   When you find an animal that appeals to you, ask to see him ridden first. Then if you like what you see, try him yourself. He should stay at a walk until asked to change gait – a horse that is constantly pulling may look showy, but is no pleasure to ride for very long. Sluggishness should also be avoided – it is discouraging work to make a listless horse respond. The goal is an alert but obedient animal. (Remember to take into consideration the time of year in which you are trying out the horse, if he is a stranger to you. The most wide-awake horse in the stable may be indifferent on a hot, humid day, and the first cold snap may put new life into some old dog—temporarily.) If you plan to ride with a group of friends discover how your prospective mount behaves with other horses. He may be quite docile by himself, but obsessed with an urge to kick any horse that comes into his vicinity.

80

Find out if the horse will back, if he leads well, if he will stand tethered, and if he will get into a horse box or trailer (you *might* want to box him some day). Ask about his disposition around the stable. Can you enter his stall safety? Does he have any vices such as cribbing (a nervous habit of chewing on the wood of his stall, not unlike fingernail biting in people).

**Physical condition**  There probably is no such thing as the perfect horse, but your horse should be serviceably sound if you are going to enjoy him. Even experienced horsemen occasionally make mistakes about soundness, so if you are genuinely interested in buying a certain animal, call in a vet to look him over, giving his opinion of the horse's suitability for your particular purpose.

**The horse's clothing**  Once you have chosen your horse, you must then buy the necessary tack and equipment. Whether you plan to keep him at a public stable or at home, you must have a 'basic wardrobe' for him. Be sure that the saddle fits both you and the horse. Saddles, even of a certain type, will vary. This is also true of the bridle; inquire as to what kind of bit or bits your horse is accustomed to. It is worth purchasing stainless steel bits as these wear much longer, and getting a good halter, since this is the piece of equipment your horse wears most. Take a rough measurement of your horse before you go shopping for blankets, since these come in different lengths, and the types which you will buy will be determined by whether you have your horse stabled or keep it at grass. Sooner or later you will need a tack trunk, to store the blankets in the summer and odd brushes and straps; they come in all sizes and prices, depending on your needs. Of course, many items in this 'basic wardrobe' are available second-hand—a good way to save money.

**Boarding your horse**  If you are not certain you can afford a horse, remember that the initial price of horse and tack is only the beginning. Unlike the family car, a horse consumes fuel even when he is not being used. Livery charges will vary according to the locality and the services you require. Training and exercising will cost more; if you are a weekend rider only, make sure your horse will be exercised daily.

Inquire about the services included in the price of the monthly board. Most stables will feed, groom, and clip your horse, clean your tack, and provide any minor medical treatment required (slight cuts, colds, etc). If

Figure 34. The bridle and bit

your horse develops a serious ailment the stable manager will call a vet – but at your expense. You will also get the bill for any tooth trouble your mount develops; in older horses sharp teeth are not uncommon and need to be 'rasped' (filed). A well-run stable will see that your horse is shod when necessary – again the bill is yours. The number of new shoes will depend upon the amount of use the horse gets and over what type of ground. Hacking on a road will wear shoes faster than riding over fields; but in any case you can safely reckon on several sets a year. (The price will vary, depending on the local blacksmith and whether your horse takes a standard shoe or has to have a custom-made one to correct a defect or enhance his way-of-going.) Most horses need their shoes reset about every six weeks. Hoofs, like fingernails, grow. The shoe is taken off, the hoof pared down, and the same shoe put back on.

**Insuring your horse**  You may decide to insure your horse; the stable will have the name of a reliable broker if you do not know one. There is, however, no way to insure a horse against accidents, lameness or illness – only death. Unless you have some high-priced breeding stock, or unless you plan to travel with your horse frequently, insurance probably is unnecessary. *But*, if you plan to let friends and neighbours ride your horse, look into liability cover for yourself. Your best friend could fall off, suffer shock, humiliation and a scratch on the arm and sue. If your best friend sues, you will probably lose, judging from cases which have come before juries.

**Home care**  Do you want to keep your horse at home and care for him yourself? Well, remember one thing: complete care will take almost all your spare time. Other than the basic wardrobe you already have acquired for your horse, he will need buckets, curry combs, brushes, a sweatscraper, water heater, clippers, saddle soap, sponges, a hoofpick, pitchfork, a shovel and a wheel-barrow. Your stable should be well ventilated without

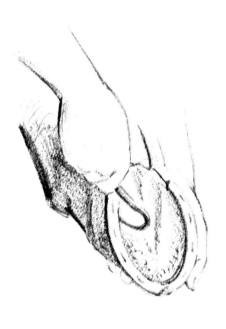

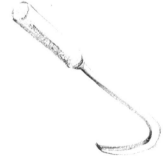

Figure 35. Cleaning the hoof

being draughty, have good drainage and floors that can be kept clean with minimum effort. You should have storage space for hay, grain and bedding (straw or shavings) and accessible water. A horse, depending on size and the season, may drink from 22 to 68 litres of water a day. Even if you have highly-desirable pasture land, grass is not enough for a healthy working horse – his diet must include oats, corn, an occasional bran mash, and of course, hay. There should be salt in his stall or pasture. The average horse, getting regular exercise, may eat between 7 to 9 kg of hay a day and hard feed according to work. Unfortunately, you cannot just toss in his ration and forget him; a horse, for his size, has a small stomach, and should be fed often. His food should be divided into three meals a day (some stables feed smaller amounts five times a day).

**A clean stable** The stable should be cleaned once a day, and picked out more often if possible. Thrush, a decay of the foot, is caused when the horse is left standing in damp, dirty bedding. The horse's hoofs of course, should be cleaned daily when he has his daily grooming. Most horses will allow you to handle their feet as long as you don't hurt them. Always start cleaning the foot around the edges – following the line of the shoe and hoof wall. The centre, frog section of the foot is more tender, and around that area work from the heel towards the point of the frog – gently.

# GROOMING YOUR HORSE

Even though you don't ride the horse every day, his coat should have some care – a once-a-week brushing leaves a dull, dandruff-infested coat. Daily grooming, even for five or ten minutes, will develop a coat with the lustre of highly polished furniture. Your stable area should have some sort of cross-tie arrangement—ropes with snaps to hook on the rings on each side of his halter. With a horse cross tied, you can work around him in

Figure 36. Grooming

safety. In cleaning, stand at his side and work from head
to tail.

You can develop ambidextrousness by starting with
the comb, brush or rag in the left hand for the head,
neck and shoulder area (when you are on his left side)
and back to the hindquarters. By standing still and using
both hands, you will not get flicked in the face by his tail
when he is chasing flies or stepped on or kicked when
he is using his hoofs for the same purpose. Get into the
habit of crossing *in front* of the horse when you want to
work on the other side.

**Seasonal problems**  Winter time grooming is more
of a problem as the coat is heavier and longer. Keeping
a horse well-blanketed will cut down on some of the
woolly growth, but come spring you will find your horse
shedding and you having more work . . . but not much

86

more if you have combed and brushed him regularly. In warm weather there is no reason why you should not give your horse a bath. Use horse shampoo and buckets of warm water. Rub him dry with rags, walk him a bit, and be sure he is not in a draught when he is put away. His tail and mane should be washed whenever they appear to need it, unless it is freezing cold. Incidently, a horse's coat will sunburn; provide cover on hot days.

## SADDLING YOUR HORSE

Once your horse is cleaned up, you are ready to ride. Put on the saddle first. As always, approach from the left side. Be certain that the girth is pulled over the top of the saddle and held on your side, lest it fly and hit the horse. Standing by his shoulder, facing his hindquarters, hold the pommel area in your left hand and the cantle

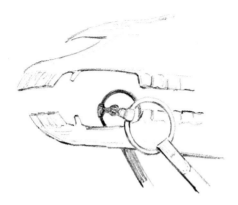

Figure 37. Positioning of bit in horse's mouth

Figure 38. Putting on the bridle

88

in your right. A flick of the wrist and the saddle is on
Once the saddle is set, it is worth the few extra steps to
walk around the other side to be sure that the girth is
flat and that none of the billet straps has twisted. Then
back on the left side, reach under and pick up the girth
and buckle it loosely and evenly. Then draw it up
gradually until you think it is as snug as it should be.
Unbuckle the halter, slip it off the horse's head and re-
buckle it around his neck. That way he is attached at
all times until you have him bridled and are ready to
mount.

## SECURING THE BRIDLE

Take the headpiece of the bridle in the right hand and
line up the bits in the left. Most horses will open their
mouths and take the bits without any trouble, but be
sure that the bits are in the mouth *before* slipping the
headpiece over the ears. If something delays you before
mounting, do *not* snap the cross ties to the bridle. Put the
halter on over the bridle and snap the ties in the accustomed rings.

## AFTER THE RIDE

After the ride, simply reverse the process. The bridle
comes off first. If you have a bucket of water handy, dip
the bit at once; this rinsing may save you some work later.
Then take off the saddle, and depending on how much
the horse is sweating, either go over him with a scraper
(same position as for cleaning) or rub him down with a rag.
You can sponge the saddle area, his nostrils and mouth
with warm water. Then, if he is still hot, put a sweat rug
or sheet on him and walk the horse slowly until he has
dried out completely and is breathing normally. Do *not*
give him water until that time. And when you lead him,
turn him around so that his head is towards the door,
and then unsnap the lead. In that way you can never be
kicked—accidently or on purpose.

While caring for your horse and attending to his bodily needs, talk to him and make much of him if he has done his job for you well. If he hasn't, try to think what you did that confused him, and still make much of him while apologising for your misdemeanour and promising better for tomorrow.

Now spare a few minutes for your tackle. Again, it will save you time in the long run. Sponge off the inside of

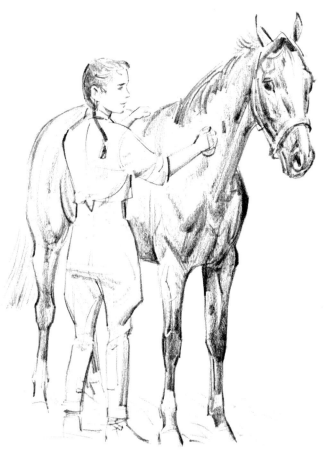

Figure 39. After the ride

the saddle – dirty, stiff saddles cause sores on the horse's back, while well-soaped saddles and bridles remain soft and flexible for years and withstand occasional rain soakings. After this give your horse his feed if he seems rested and dried off. Remember a light feed or a bran mash if he has worked really hard, hunted for example. Check two hours later to see if he is all right, refill his water and hay up for the night. Now you can sit down and relax. And if you really like your horse, and your horse likes you all this will not seem a bit like work, but rather a rewarding pleasure.

After having read this little book, and followed the suggestions, I hope both you and your mount will have many, many happy hours together.

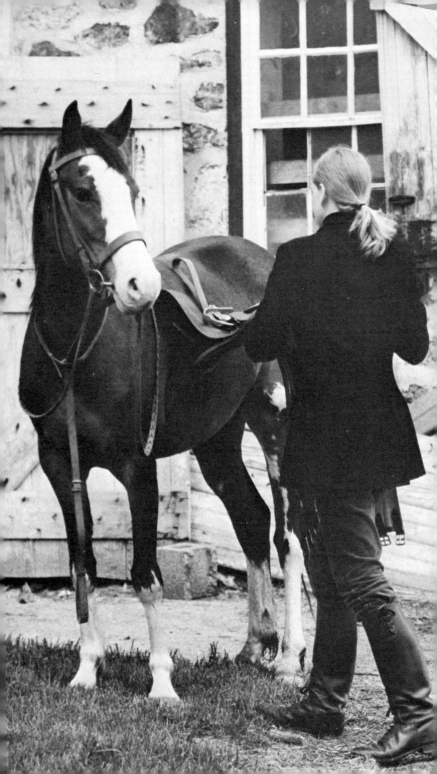

# 6 Useful Information

## ASSOCIATIONS

The British Horse Society
Sec: J E Blackmore
     National Equestrian Centre
     Stoneleigh
     Kenilworth
     Warwickshire CV8 2LR

Parent body of the Pony Club and all affiliated Riding Clubs. The Society's main aims are to guard the welfare and interests of both horses and riders, and to work for the expansion and improvement of riding facilities throughout the country.

The Pony Club
Sec: Miss C Moir
     National Equestrian Centre
     Stoneleigh
     Kenilworth
     Warwickshire CV8 2LR

Encourages young people to ride, and membership is open to everyone under the age of 19. Full details of club activities will be supplied upon request.

93

Ponies of Britain
Sec: Mrs G Spooner
      Brookside Farm
      Ascot
      Berkshire SL5 7LU

Concerned with the promotion of the well being of ponies everywhere. Publishes an annual list of Approved Centres for Trekking and Riding Holidays.

Association of British Riding Schools
Sec: Mrs M Simlo
      Chesham House
      56 Green End Road
      Sawtry
      Cambridgeshire PE17 5UY

Issues annually a Handbook of Approved Members.

Riding for the Disabled Association
Sec: Miss C Haynes
      National Equestrian Centre
      Stoneleigh
      Kenilworth
      Warwickshire CV8 2LR

The Association has over 240 member groups throughout the country.

The National Pony Society
Sec: Cmdr B H Brown RN
      85 Cliddesden Road
      Basingstoke
      Hants RG21 3HA

Maintains a Stud Book and Register of Riding Ponies, and provides information, help and advice on all matters connected with ponies.

It is important to remember that after opening a gate you should close it
properly, to protect other livestock from straying

# BOOK LIST

Books – general and specialist interest

The British Horse Society and the Pony Club will supply
lists of publications upon request. The following, published
by the BHS, are of especial interest to the beginner:

*The Safety Code for Riding* (free).
*The Riding Code* (free).
*Freedom to Ride* (free).
*Where to Ride – List of Approved Riding Establishments.*

J A Allen & Company Ltd
1 Lower Grosvenor Place
London SW1W 0EL

offer the finest selection of books on riding, and will supply
an up-to-date catalogue upon request. A wide range of
topics is covered, including:

*Feeding Ponies* by Professor W C Miller.
*Showing Ponies* by Ann Bullen.
*The Pony Rider's Book* by George Wheatley.
*Teaching the Child Rider* by Pamela J Roberts.
*The Occasional Horseman* by George Canning.

*All about Horses in the South* by James Dunning (Heritage
Publications), available from W H Smith. A useful guide
to where to ride, where to watch.

Magazines – general interest

*Horse + Pony* (Scottish Farmer Publications Ltd) monthly.
*Pony* (D J Murphy (Publishers) Ltd) monthly.
*Riding* (IPC Magazines Ltd) monthly.

Magazines – specialist interest

*Equitation* (BHA (Publications) Ltd) monthly. Training
horse and rider, including dressage.
*Light Horse* (D J Murphy (Publishers) Ltd) monthly. In-
cludes eventing, hunters and point-to-point.
*Stable Management* (Riding School and Stable Management Ltd) 6 a year. Management of stables and care of
horses.
*Stud and Stable* (Stud & Stable Ltd) monthly. For owners,
trainers and riders of thoroughbred horses.